Original title:

Enlightened Love Practices

Author: Kalle Soosalu

ISBN HARDBACK: 978-9916-87-138-6

ISBN PAPERBACK: 978-9916-87-139-3

ISBN EBOOK: 978-9916-87-140-9

Seeds of Transformative Tenderness

In a garden where whispers bloom,
Soft touches greet the quiet loom.
Hearts mend like vines, entwined in trust,
Tenderness births life from gentle dust.

With every seed, a promise sways,
Sunlight dances on hopeful days.
Roots dig deep in the soil of care,
Transforming sorrows into shared air.

Raindrops fall like laughter shared,
Nurturing love that's freely bared.
Hearts grow strong, as seasons blend,
In this haven, wounds learn to mend.

A tapestry of colors bright,
Weaving souls in shared delight.
Together we rise, forever free,
In this garden, just you and me.

Fires of Passion in Kindred Spirits

Two flames that flicker, dancing close,
In the night, where warmth engrosses.
Hearts collide in a fervent blaze,
Fueling love in a wild maze.

Kindred spirits, a force so rare,
Igniting sparks in the scented air.
With every glance, the world ignites,
Passion throbs on starry nights.

Through trials faced, we brightly burn,
Every twist, a lesson learned.
In the heat of love, we boldly stand,
Together forging, hand in hand.

Like embers glowing in the dark,
Our souls unite, a fervent spark.
Fires of passion, forever untamed,
In this dance, we are unashamed.

Hearts in Unity

Two souls entwined beneath the stars,
A bond unbroken, no matter the scars.
With every heartbeat, a rhythm divine,
Together we flourish, our spirits align.

In laughter we dance, in silence we grow,
A testament found in the love that we know.
Side by side, we weather the storm,
In hearts united, we always stay warm.

Illuminating Spaces Between

In the quiet whispers of early dawn,
Your presence lingers, though you are gone.
Light threads of memories, softly they weave,
Illuminated truths that we both believe.

Glimmers of hope in the shadows we cast,
Together we're stronger, our love unsurpassed.
Through every dark hour, a flicker shines bright,
Guiding us onward, our infinite light.

Love Like a Gentle Flame

It flickers softly, this love that we share,
A warmth that envelops, a tender care.
With every whisper, it swells and it glows,
In its quiet embrace, our connection grows.

Not fierce like fire, but steady and true,
In the dance of the embers, it's me and you.
A beacon of solace when days turn to night,
Love like a gentle flame, forever alight.

The Portrait of Mutual Care

With every brushstroke, our story unfolds,
A canvas of moments, a masterpiece told.
Each color a heartbeat, each line a decree,
In the portrait of love, it's just you and me.

Through trials and triumphs, hand in hand, we stand,
In the gallery of life, a beautiful band.
Together we cherish, through laughter and tears,
The artistry crafted throughout all the years.

The Mirror of Compassionate Hearts

In the depth of silent gaze,
Reflections dance in gentle ways.
A kindred spirit, soft and bright,
Embracing shadows with the light.

With every tear a story weaves,
A tapestry of hopes and leaves.
Together strong, we face the day,
In gratitude, we find our way.

A hand extended, warm and true,
The mirror shows the best of you.
In love's embrace, we find our place,
Compassion blooms, a tender grace.

Through storms that test, and winds that blow,
The heart remembers what to show.
In kindness found, our spirits soar,
The mirror shines forevermore.

Lights of Sacred Companionship

In every laugh a light ignites,
A beacon glowing through the nights.
Together we navigate the maze,
Illuminating all our days.

In quiet moments side by side,
We find a warmth that will abide.
A bond unspoken, yet so clear,
In sacred trust, we draw near.

Through shadows cast, our spirits gleam,
We share the hope and weave the dream.
In unity, we softly shine,
As lights of love, your heart in mine.

In laughter, tears, in joy and strife,
Companionship enriches life.
Together we shall rise, ascend,
In every heart, a cherished friend.

The Essence of Nurturing Bonds

In gentle whispers, roots entwine,
A garden blooms where hearts align.
With every gesture, seeds are sown,
In nurturing, our love has grown.

Through trials faced and lessons learned,
The warmth of care, forever burned.
In tender moments, life unfolds,
A story rich with hearts of gold.

From laughter shared to quiet sighs,
The essence lives beneath the skies.
In every hug, a promise made,
In nurturing, love is displayed.

Together we shall weather storms,
In bonds so strong, we take our forms.
With roots so deep, our branches sway,
In nurturing love, we'll find our way.

Amulets of Mutual Growth

In every challenge, wisdom blooms,
With lessons learned, the spirit fumes.
Together we shall rise and thrive,
As amulets, we come alive.

Through sacred trust, we build the path,
Transforming trials into laughter's math.
In unity, our dreams take flight,
As endless stars adorn the night.

With every step, we nurture more,
A journey shared, a heart to soar.
In mutual growth, we intertwine,
As trees that bear the sweetest vine.

In moments crafted, love will show,
The beauty of the seeds we sow.
As amulets that shine and gleam,
Together we ignite the dream.

The Language of Unspoken Bonds

In silence deep, our hearts align,
A glance, a touch, a shared design.
Words unneeded, truth resides,
In every pulse, our love confides.

Through tangled thoughts and dreams we weave,
Connections strong, we can't deceive.
With every sigh, the bonds renew,
In wordless depths, I find you true.

Ethereal Threads of Union

A whisper faint, a spirit's thread,
Binding us close, though words are dead.
In shadows cast, we dance in light,
Ethereal ties that soar in flight.

Fleeting glances, gentle grace,
We share a world, an endless space.
In every heartbeat, echoes ring,
A symphony of love we sing.

Blossoms of Understanding

In gardens lush, we softly bloom,
Petals bright dispel the gloom.
Each quiet nod, each smile so wide,
Nurtures trust that won't subside.

Through storms and sun, our roots entwine,
Blossoms flourish, sweet and fine.
In fragrance shared, our souls unite,
A dance of love, a pure delight.

Gentle Currents of Affection

In rivers soft, our feelings flow,
Winding paths where feelings grow.
With every wave, compassion swells,
In gentle tides, our story dwells.

The currents sway with tender care,
Love's embrace, a silent prayer.
Through ebbs and flows, we find the way,
In quiet strength, forever stay.

Stars Beneath Our Skin

In the night, secrets glow,
Whispers of dreams that flow.
Light and shadow intertwine,
Dancing softly, hearts align.

Every heartbeat, a twinkle bright,
Echoes of stars igniting the night.
We carry galaxies within,
The universe starts from within.

Tides of Compassion

Waves caress the sandy shore,
Gifts of kindness we explore.
In each swell, love's embrace,
Healing hearts, a sacred space.

Together, we rise and fall,
Carried by compassion's call.
In the depths, we find our way,
Guided by compassion's sway.

Harmonies of the Heart

Melodies weave through the air,
Notes of love beyond compare.
In each silence, a refrain,
Bringing joy, easing pain.

Together, our voices blend,
Creating notes that transcend.
Sweet chords of unity play,
Binding hearts in perfect sway.

The Dance of Kindred Spirits

Underneath the silver moon,
Spirits twirl to a gentle tune.
With each step, a story told,
In the dance, we break the mold.

Hands entwined, we leap and spin,
In this rhythm, we begin.
Kindred souls, forever free,
Swaying to eternity.

Navigating the Sea of Togetherness

In the waves we find our place,
A shared journey, an endless space.
With hands clasped tight, we brave the tide,
In the sea of love, we confide.

Beneath the stars, our dreams align,
Charting paths where hearts entwine.
Each whisper soft, a gentle guide,
Together, our spirits ride.

The compass turns, the sails unfurl,
In every storm, we share the whirl.
With every crest and every fall,
We gather strength, we stand tall.

Through tranquil nights and sunny days,
Together, we'll find our ways.
In this vast sea, we'll always be,
Navigating love, you and me.

Paths Interwoven in Light

In the garden of our shared dreams,
We walk together, or so it seems.
With every step, a story we write,
Paths interwoven, bathed in light.

Beneath the branches, shadows play,
We find our peace in the gentle sway.
Each laughter shared, a soft embrace,
In every moment, we find our place.

When the night falls, stars shine bright,
Guiding us through the waning light.
We carve our names in the sands of time,
With every heartbeat, a new rhyme.

Together we'll walk, hand in hand,
In this beautiful, timeless land.
With hearts aglow, our spirits bright,
We'll cherish our paths interwoven in light.

Whispers of the Heart's Awakening

In silence deep, a whisper stirs,
The heart awakens, as longing purrs.
With every breath, a secret sigh,
In the stillness, love's first cry.

Beneath the moon's soft, tender gaze,
We find ourselves in a gentle haze.
Each heartbeat sings a cryptic tune,
Together we dance beneath the moon.

Voices soft, like summer's breeze,
In their embrace, we find our ease.
Every look, a story told,
In whispers shared, our hearts unfold.

Awakening dreams, like petals new,
In the garden of feelings, just us two.
Together we rise, in soft release,
With every whisper, we find our peace.

The Dance of Soulful Connections

In the twilight, shadows blend,
A sacred space where hearts transcend.
With gentle grace, our spirits twine,
In this dance, your soul meets mine.

Fleeting glances, a knowing smile,
In every step, we reconcile.
With rhythm sweet, our hearts will sway,
In this moment, I long to stay.

Music plays, the night ignites,
Two souls merging in dazzling lights.
Each twirl a promise, spoken true,
In the dance of souls, I choose you.

With every beat, a story shared,
In this embrace, we're unprepared.
Together we whirl, lost in the trance,
In the dance of life, we take a chance.

Melodies of Entwined Lives

In the dance of time, we sway,
Notes of laughter, soft and bright.
Each heartbeat sings, come what may,
Together we weave day and night.

Through storms and skies that brightly glow,
With every step, our spirits climb.
In whispered dreams, love's river flows,
Melodies sweet, a shared rhyme.

Like vines entwined beneath the sun,
Our joys and sorrows intertwine.
In this vast world, we are not done,
Creating life, both yours and mine.

Together we'll pen our own song,
With every note, our essence free.
In harmony, we both belong,
Entwined in life's sweet symphony.

The Warm Embrace of Harmonious Hearts

In the still of night, we find peace,
A warmth that wraps both near and far.
In tender moments, troubles cease,
Our hearts aligned, a guiding star.

With every hug, our worries fade,
Like whispers shared in soft moonlight.
In gentle touch, love's truths displayed,
A bond that grows with pure delight.

Through laughter shared and tears we shed,
In every heartbeat's gentle thrum.
In love's embrace, we both are led,
A place where weary souls feel home.

The world may shift and shadows cast,
Yet here we stand, embraced and whole.
In harmonious hearts, love will last,
A symphony that soothes the soul.

Unity Through Compassionate Presence

In silence shared, we weave our strength,
Compassion blooms in every glance.
Together, we go any length,
In unity, we find our chance.

With kindness sown, a garden grows,
In every deed, the heart expands.
Through trials faced, our spirit knows,
Together we shall take firm stands.

A gentle touch in times of need,
Our presence felt, a healing balm.
In every word, a loving seed,
We nurture peace, our iron calm.

Compassionate hearts in the fray,
Embracing all, both weak and bold.
In unity, we find our way,
A tapestry of love untold.

Chasing the Light Together

In dawn's embrace, we rise anew,
With dreams as vast as open skies.
Hand in hand, the path we pursue,
In pursuit of truth, our spirits fly.

Through shadowed valleys, we break free,
With courage found in each dear glance.
Chasing the light, just you and me,
In every step, we take our chance.

The world may shift, and dark clouds loom,
Yet with our laughter, skies will clear.
In every moment, love will bloom,
Together, we dispel the fear.

In twilight's glow, our dreams ignite,
A journey forged of hearts so bright.
With every breath, we dance in light,
Chasing our dreams, forever bright.

The Dance of Resilient Trust

In shadows deep, we find our way,
With every step, come what may.
Through storms that rage, and doubts that churn,
A bond is forged, and hearts will learn.

With each embrace, a silent pact,
In honest words, there's no abstract.
We rise anew, hand in hand,
In the dance of life, we take a stand.

Like rivers flow, our faith runs strong,
In harmony, we sing our song.
Stumbling paths may blur our sight,
Yet trust remains, our guiding light.

So let us twirl, through thick and thin,
In this dance of trust, we both win.
Together we weave, the fragile thread,
A story of hope, where fears are shed.

Whispered Secrets of Affection

In twilight hues, your voice I hear,
Soft melodies that draw me near.
With every word, a gentle caress,
In whispered secrets, love's finesse.

Beneath the stars, our hearts entwined,
In sacred whispers, souls aligned.
Each secret shared, a treasure true,
An endless bond, just me and you.

With tender smiles, we thread the night,
In quiet moments, pure delight.
Through laughter's glow and soothing sighs,
Our hidden truths shall never die.

In every glance, affection blooms,
A language sweet that softly looms.
Together we craft a world so rare,
In whispered secrets, we're laid bare.

Transcendent Threads of Connection

In silent glances, worlds collide,
Threads of fate, we cannot hide.
Through woven paths and serendipity,
In every heartbeat, you're part of me.

We dance as one, through time and space,
Embracing all, in love's embrace.
With every story, a thread we weave,
In moments shared, we both believe.

Like constellations across the night,
We shine together, pure and bright.
A tapestry rich, each color sings,
In connection deep, our spirits take wings.

Let us explore this sacred bond,
In transcendent threads, we are so fond.
With open hearts, the journey flows,
In union strong, our love just grows.

Hearts in Gentle Alignment

In quiet moments, we find our peace,
Hearts in tune, our worries cease.
With breaths unspoken, silence speaks,
In gentle rhythms, love uniquely peaks.

Through trials faced, we navigate,
In steadfast trust, we resonate.
With hands entwined, we boldly strive,
In hearts aligned, we feel alive.

Every heartbeat, a steady guide,
With you beside, I cast aside.
In harmony's embrace, we create,
A life that sings, a love innate.

As stars above join in the dance,
In gentle alignment, we take our chance.
Together we stand, against the tide,
In love's own journey, forever side by side.

Touching the Infinite Mirror

In stillness, reflections lie,
A gaze into the endless sky.
Each thought, a ripple in the glass,
Time dances softly, moments pass.

The truth unfolds in silent hues,
In whispers only the heart can use.
Fragments of dreams, a cosmic trail,
Guiding us where spirits sail.

Echoes of love in every shard,
Binding souls, though times are hard.
Through shadows cast, a light shines bright,
Uniting worlds in pure delight.

In the mirror, we find our fate,
Infinite paths that intertwine and await.
Each connection, a thread of gold,
Woven stories yet to be told.

Shimmering Pathways of Trust

Beneath the stars, we find our way,
A gentle map where hearts can sway.
Each step we take, a soft embrace,
Trust weaves through time and space.

Along the paths, the shadows gleam,
A tapestry of shared esteem.
In every glance, a promise made,
Bridges built that will not fade.

When storms arise and doubts take flight,
We'll hold on tight, in darkest night.
Creating light from what we share,
Together, love conquers despair.

With every breath, our bond will grow,
In shimmering trust, we'll always know.
Hand in hand, we'll face the test,
In the dance of life, we find our rest.

Dancing Shadows of Affection

Underneath the moonlit glow,
Two shadows sense the ebb and flow.
In quiet moves, our spirits twirl,
A symphony of love unfurl.

Each heartbeat drums a sweet refrain,
A melody that speaks our name.
In silence, whispers softly fade,
As warmth and trust serenely invade.

With every pause, a moment savored,
In tender glances, affection flavored.
Together in this sacred space,
Our souls entwined, an endless grace.

Through shadows cast and light embraced,
We find a dance that can't be replaced.
In every step, love's joy is shown,
Two hearts as one, forever grown.

The Art of Unified Presence

In the stillness, we arrive,
Two souls awake, feeling alive.
Our breaths align, a rhythmic beat,
In shared silence, our hearts meet.

Each moment holds a sacred light,
Guiding us through day and night.
In unity, we find our song,
A place where we both belong.

Hands intertwined, our spirits dance,
In the essence of a single glance.
Time melts away, all else falls,
In this art, true presence calls.

Together we craft a masterpiece,
With every heartbeat, every crease.
In love's embrace, we find our truth,
The art of life, forever youth.

Celestial Stars of Heart Connection

In the night sky, we find our thread,
Twinkling lights where dreams are fed.
Hearts align in silent grace,
Connected souls in a vast space.

Guided by the stars above,
An invisible bond, pure as love.
Through galaxies, hand in hand,
Together strong, we make our stand.

Each heartbeat syncs to the celestial tune,
In the universe, we are one, not two.
Let whispers float on the cosmic breeze,
United forever, with souls at ease.

The Tuning Fork of Kindred Spirits

In the quiet hum of the night,
Resonance captures pure delight.
A gentle strike, our hearts align,
Kindred spirits, yours and mine.

With every note, we find our way,
Echoes of love in the light of day.
Together we sing a timeless song,
In harmony, where we belong.

Vibrations dance on the air we share,
A sacred bond, beyond compare.
In this symphony of hearts so true,
The tuning fork knows me and you.

A Garden of Illuminated Affections

Within the garden, blooms so bright,
Petals glimmer in the soft twilight.
Laughter mingles with fragrant air,
Illuminated hearts blossom fair.

Every glance, a flower in bloom,
In this haven, love dispels the gloom.
Roots intertwine beneath the ground,
In this space, our joy is found.

Seasons change, yet we remain,
Nurtured by sunshine, blessed by rain.
Together we cultivate our dreams,
In love's garden, life redeems.

Resonant Waves of Caring

Waves of compassion crash on shores,
Carrying whispers, opening doors.
In the tides of our shared embrace,
Finding comfort in every place.

The ocean's depth holds secrets true,
In currents strong, I reach for you.
Together we navigate life's sea,
Resonant waves, just you and me.

With every surge, our spirits rise,
In caring waves, no disguise.
Through storms and calm, we will sail,
On love's vast ocean, we shall prevail.

Synchronous Hearts in Timeless Dance

In quiet halls where whispers glide,
Two souls entwined, no need to hide.
Their hearts beat soft, a gentle tune,
In sync they move, beneath the moon.

With every glance, the world does fade,
In perfect rhythm, a bond is made.
Each step they take, a story spun,
A dance for two, forever one.

In swirls of joy, their laughter rings,
Echoing sweetly, the love it brings.
A timeless waltz through night and day,
In synchronous hearts, they'll find their way.

Through fleeting time, their spirits soar,
Together strong, they seek no more.
In every twirl, both lost and found,
Their love's the music, the sweetest sound.

Petals of Connection

From seed to bloom, a journey starts,
In gentle gardens, grow our hearts.
Each petal soft, a touch divine,
In fragrant dreams, your hand in mine.

Like morning dew on blades of grass,
Our moments shine, together pass.
In every hue, a story told,
The warmth of love that never grows old.

With whispers sweet, the flowers sway,
In nature's grace, we find our way.
As sunshine spills on fields so wide,
In petals soft, our souls abide.

For every storm that comes and goes,
Our roots run deep, the heart still knows.
In vibrant blooms, we'll always stand,
Together joined, in love's sweet hand.

The Symphony of Intimacy Revealed

Within the notes, our secrets dwell,
A symphony that weaves its spell.
In harmony, our voices rise,
Awakening dreams beneath the skies.

Each soft crescendo, a tender touch,
In melodies, we share so much.
The world may fade, but we remain,
In tender chords, through joy and pain.

With every heartbeat, the rhythm flows,
In whispered tales, our passion grows.
The timbre of our souls entwined,
In every note, true love defined.

As silence breaks, together strong,
In quiet depths, where we belong.
Our symphony, a bond revealed,
In every moment, love's magic healed.

A Tapestry of Shared Journeys

In threads of gold, our paths are spun,
With every weave, two lives as one.
The stories told in colors bright,
A tapestry of love and light.

Through valleys deep and mountains high,
We'll trace the trails beneath the sky.
With hands united, we'll face the day,
In every stitch, we find our way.

From morning's rise to evening's close,
A woven tale as life bestows.
In laughter's thread, in sorrows shared,
Each moment cherished, deeply cared.

As time unfolds, our fabric grows,
In every heart, the love it shows.
A tapestry rich, in joy and strife,
Together we embark on this journey of life.

Radiance in Togetherness

In the glow of shared laughter,
Hearts intertwine like vines.
Each moment, a warm chapter,
In this journey, love shines.

With every touch, we blossom,
Like petals in spring's embrace.
Together, we find our freedom,
In unity, we find our place.

The world fades; it's just us,
In this cocoon of dreams.
Trust flows without a fuss,
Together, we are beams.

Radiance that we foster,
In our shared endeavor.
Every day, we grow closer,
In this love, we are forever.

Unfolding the Light Within

When silence holds a whisper,
Dreams begin to take flight.
Layers peel back, crisper,
Revealing our inner light.

A spark ignites our being,
Guided by the moon's glow.
In stillness, we are seeing,
The beauty that we sow.

With each breath, we discover,
Our souls, a radiant hue.
In ourselves, we recover,
And shine in all we do.

Together, we are stronger,
Unfolding what's within.
In this journey, we wander,
Finding where love begins.

Harmonies of Compassionate Souls

In the echoes of kindness,
Voices blend like the sea.
Each note rich with mindfulness,
Creating unity.

Through trials and the laughter,
We weave a tender song.
In each heart, a chapter,
Where we all belong.

The world sings of connection,
As compassion lights the way.
In shared love's reflection,
We shine brighter each day.

Together, we are dancing,
In this soulful embrace.
Harmonies enhancing,
Hope transcending time and space.

Threads of Affection Illuminated

Woven softly, our stories,
Threads glowing in the night.
Each tale lit with glories,
Bringing warmth and delight.

In the fabric of our hearts,
Love's colors intertwine.
From each seam, joy imparts,
Showing how we align.

Through the storms, we gather,
Stitching hope with our hands.
In each other's laughter,
We create peaceful lands.

These threads, forever anchored,
In the loom of our lives.
Affection, brightly spangled,
Illuminates as it thrives.

Luminescence in Every Embrace

In twilight's hue, we find our way,
With whispers soft, the shadows sway.
Your laughter sparkles, pure and bright,
A warmth that spills through the quiet night.

We dance in circles, hearts in flight,
Through tangled paths, we seek the light.
Each touch ignites, a flickering flame,
In this communion, we're never the same.

Veils of silence, holding truths,
In every gaze, the depths of youth.
With each embrace, the world stands still,
In crystalline moments, we find our will.

Together we glow, an endless dream,
In every heartbeat, a shared theme.
Luminescence woven in each kiss,
A tapestry of love, a boundless bliss.

Elysian Bonds of Understanding

In gardens lush where whisper flows,
Two souls entwined, their story grows.
With gentle words, we break the wall,
In every heartbeat, hear the call.

Across the skies, our spirits soar,
In sacred spaces, we seek for more.
The truth unfolds in tender grace,
In shared glances, we find our place.

Through trials faced, we find our might,
In darkest hours, we're each other's light.
With every word, our hearts align,
In bonds of trust, our love will shine.

Elysian paths that intertwine,
A bond so deep, it feels divine.
Together we rise, unwavering, grand,
In the soil of hope, together we stand.

Awakening the Heart's Wisdom

In quiet moments, truth appears,
The heart speaks soft, dissolving fears.
With every beat, wisdom unfolds,
A map to life in stories told.

We wander through the fields of time,
Each lesson learned, a silent rhyme.
The stars above our guide so bright,
In shadows cast, we find our light.

With open palms, we greet the dawn,
Awakening dreams, reborn, withdrawn.
In nature's cradle, we find our song,
Through seasons' change, we still belong.

The heart's wisdom, a treasure vast,
A journey long, from first to last.
Together we grow, resilient, wise,
In each connection, the soul's rise.

The Sacred Geometry of Us

In every angle, love takes form,
A sacred dance, both bright and warm.
Shapes of passion, lines of grace,
In every curve, we find our place.

With every heartbeat, patterns weave,
In layered silence, we believe.
The universe maps our intertwined fate,
In cosmic art, there's never late.

Circles of trust, triangles of care,
In the symphony of us, beauty's rare.
We sketch our dreams with gentle hands,
In colors bright, our love withstands.

The canvas stretches, time unfolds,
In unity, our story holds.
The sacred geometry in every breath,
In love's embrace, we conquer death.

The Echo of Together

In laughter we find our way,
A dance of souls in bright ballet.
In quiet whispers, hearts unite,
Together we shine, a guiding light.

Through storms that test our frail resolve,
Hand in hand, our fears dissolve.
In every moment, bonds grow strong,
Together we write a timeless song.

From valleys deep to mountains high,
We chase the dreams that touch the sky.
In echoes of love, we learn to soar,
Together we rise, forevermore.

Each step we take, a story spun,
In the fabric of us, we're never done.
In every chapter, joy and strife,
Together we weave the tale of life.

Moments of Grace and Giving

In small gestures, kindness blooms,
A soft light breaking through the glooms.
Each smile shared, a gift to keep,
Moments of grace, so pure and deep.

With open hearts, we freely give,
In every touch, we learn to live.
Through acts of love, the world expands,
In unity, we join our hands.

With every sunrise, mercy wakes,
In gentle waves, our spirit shakes.
In fleeting seconds, infinite trust,
Moments we treasure, a must.

When shadows linger, hope will rise,
In faith and warmth, we find the prize.
Together we stand, the journey's aim,
Moments of grace, we'll gladly claim.

From Shadows to Sunlight

In whispered doubts, the shadows creep,
Yet in the dark, dreams start to leap.
With every struggle, we learn to fight,
From shadows we grow, step into light.

In every fear, a lesson lies,
A chance to rise and claim the skies.
Through trials faced, our spirits soar,
From shadows to sunlight, we explore.

With courage found in depths of night,
We gather strength, prepare for flight.
In brighter days, our hearts ignite,
From shadows to sunlight, pure delight.

Hand in hand, we chase the dawn,
In unity, a new world drawn.
Together we shine, a radiant sight,
From shadows to sunlight, hearts in flight.

The Canvas of Shared Dreams

On canvas wide, our visions blend,
In strokes of hope, the colors mend.
With every heartbeat, dreams take shape,
The canvas alive, our spirits escape.

In hues of laughter, shades of care,
We craft a story woven rare.
With brushes dipped in love's embrace,
The canvas of dreams, a sacred space.

In every flaw, a beauty lies,
Together we paint our endless skies.
With every challenge, new colors stream,
The canvas expands, fulfilling our dream.

As brush meets canvas, fate takes flight,
In shared creation, day turns to night.
A masterpiece born from heart's esteem,
The canvas reflects our cherished dream.

Sacred Rituals of Kindred Spirits

In quiet woods where whispers dwell,
We gather close, the heart will swell.
With gentle hands, we weave a thread,
Of stories shared, where love is fed.

Beneath the stars, our voices blend,
A sacred bond that shall not end.
In laughter bright, in silence deep,
In every promise, our souls we keep.

Rituals crafted in soft moonlight,
We dance with shadows, hearts in flight.
With every step, the spirits rise,
In kinship found, our spirits wise.

Eternal flames burn in the night,
Together bound, we are the light.
With open arms, we greet the dawn,
In sacred love, we journey on.

Embracing the Divine Union

Two hearts entwined, a sacred spark,
In every glance, ignites the dark.
With breath held close, we lean and sway,
In this embrace, we find our way.

Under the gaze of watchful skies,
We merge as one, where stillness lies.
In every heartbeat, a song is sung,
The universe hums, our anthem sprung.

Fingers interlace, a gentle hold,
Our love, a story yet untold.
With every kiss, the worlds align,
In sacred bonds, your soul meets mine.

Through trials faced and joys we share,
In every challenge, we lay bare.
Together, strong, we rise above,
Embracing all, we find our love.

Heartbeats in Sacred Rhythm

In quiet moments, hearts align,
With every pulse, a dance divine.
The world around us fades away,
In sacred rhythm, here we stay.

Whispers shared in twilight's glow,
A symphony that softly flows.
Beneath the moon, we feel the beat,
Two souls in sync, our love complete.

The path is woven with threads of gold,
In sacred breaths, our stories told.
With every glance, a quiet hymn,
In heartbeats shared, we live within.

Together we soar, through highs and lows,
In harmony, the love that grows.
Let echoes linger in the night,
In sacred rhythm, hearts take flight.

The Alchemy of Shared Dreams

In twilight's fold, we weave our dreams,
With passion's fire, the starlight gleams.
Together we shape the night's embrace,
In alchemy, we find our place.

With whispered hopes, we craft the light,
In every shadow, our vision bright.
Through the mists, our spirits glide,
In sacred trust, forever side by side.

Through trials faced and joy reclaimed,
In every heartbeat, we're unashamed.
In love's embrace, our dreams unite,
A masterpiece against the night.

With open hearts, we share the weight,
In every moment, we shape our fate.
Through dreams achieved and those yet born,
Together, forever, a new dawn is sworn.

Vessels of Warm Connectivity

Across the seas, our spirits sail,
Bound by whispers, we shall prevail.
Hearts entwined, a gentle thread,
In laughter's glow, all fears are shed.

Through stormy nights, we find our way,
Unified by love, come what may.
With every touch, a spark ignites,
In this embrace, we reach new heights.

Each story shared, a bridge we build,
In silent moments, our hearts are filled.
Together we rise, without a fight,
Vessels of warmth, a guiding light.

In every tear, there's hope reborn,
In unison's arms, we break the dawn.
Connected forever, hand in hand,
We'll navigate life, a vibrant band.

The Bridge of Understanding

In the quiet space, we often meet,
Where words are sparse, yet hearts compete.
Listening deeply, we seek the truth,
In gentle exchanges, reclaim our youth.

Bridges built on respect and grace,
In every glance, our souls embrace.
Differences fade when hearts unite,
In the warmth of empathy's light.

Through open minds, ideas fly,
In shared moments, we soar high.
Where once was doubt, now blooms the trust,
Understanding thrives, as it must.

Together we stand, side by side,
In this connection, we shall abide.
The bridge of love will never rust,
In unity's strength, we place our trust.

Ripples of Joyful Affection

In laughter's echo, joy takes flight,
Ripples of love, a pure delight.
With every smile, we share our heat,
In simple moments, our spirits meet.

Through every hug, warm hearts align,
In gentle kindness, our souls intertwine.
Like ripples spreading on a stream,
Affection flows like a cherished dream.

With every gesture, we plant a seed,
In joy's embrace, there's no need for greed.
Together we create a vibrant hue,
Brightening the world in all we do.

For every tear, we find a way,
Transforming sorrow into play.
With joyful affection, we uplift,
In these ripples, we find our gift.

Source of Endless Light in Unity

In shadows cast, we find our glow,
A light that shines, a vibrant show.
Together we rise, our spirits bright,
Source of endless love, pure and white.

Through trials faced, we stand as one,
In unity's embrace, we've just begun.
With every challenge, our light expands,
Illuminating paths with caring hands.

In silent moments, truth resides,
Guiding our hearts like ocean tides.
Each flicker sparks a deeper bond,
In this connection, we learn to respond.

Together we weave a tapestry,
Of countless dreams, in harmony.
Source of endless light, we ignite,
In unity's love, we take flight.

Soulful Journeys of Intimacy

In quiet whispers, hearts unfold,
Secrets shared, like stories told.
Two souls intertwined, time stands still,
Embracing warmth, a shared thrill.

Beneath the stars, we lay in trust,
Every touch, a gentle must.
Echoes of laughter, joy of our song,
In the tapestry of us, we belong.

In shadows deep, we find the light,
Together we dance, through day and night.
With every glance, a promise made,
In this journey, we are unafraid.

Beyond the distance, our spirits soar,
In soulful journeys, we seek more.
Through the storms and skies so blue,
In intimacy, I find you.

Kindness in Each Breath

In every heartbeat, kindness flows,
Like gentle rivers, it ebbs and grows.
A smile exchanged on a busy street,
In tiny gestures, our souls meet.

With every breath, compassion sings,
A thread of love, connecting things.
In moments shared, we plant the seeds,
Of hope and healing, fulfilling needs.

Through every trial, we lend a hand,
United, together, we make our stand.
In the quiet acts, our spirits thrive,
In kindness, we feel truly alive.

A world brightened with each shared grace,
In every heart, find a warm place.
With every dawn, let kindness reign,
In each breath taken, love remains.

A Symphony of Shared Moments

In the laughter that fills the air,
A melody sweet, beyond compare.
With every glance, a note we play,
Creating symphonies day by day.

Time stands still in a warm embrace,
Every moment, a tender space.
The rhythm of hearts, in sync they beat,
In shared moments, life feels complete.

In silence speaking, we know the score,
In joyful chords, our spirits soar.
With shared memories, the music grows,
In this orchestra of love, we compose.

Through every trial, through every cheer,
Our song remains, forever near.
A symphony played, in the light we bask,
In each shared moment, love is the task.

Radiance in Vulnerability

In the cracks of silence, truth does shine,
In open hearts, we cross the line.
Bare souls dancing, in the light,
Radiance found, through shared fright.

With every story, a thread of gold,
In vulnerability, we are bold.
Each scar a testament, each tear a song,
In this rawness, we feel we belong.

Naked souls, unmasked and free,
In our frailty, strength we see.
As shadows linger and fears arise,
In vulnerability, love never lies.

Together we rise, in depths we tread,
Radiance glowing, where hope is spread.
In every heartbeat, we learn to trust,
In vulnerability, we are unjust.

Brightening Shadows into Shared Light

In the hush of the night, we find our way,
Whispers of comfort lead us to stay.
Through tangled fears, we gently tread,
Lighting the path where our hearts can be led.

Together we rise, in the softest embrace,
Casting aside all the doubts that we face.
With every soft laugh that dances on air,
We blend our shadows, a tapestry rare.

As dawn draws near, the colors ignite,
Awakening dreams in the morning light.
We share our stories, swap tales from the past,
In this woven moment, we feel free at last.

United in spirit, two souls intertwine,
Creating a warmth that endlessly shines.
From shadows of sorrow, we bravely take flight,
Transforming our journey into shared light.

A Journey through Interwoven Souls

Two paths converge on this winding road,
Hearts find their rhythm, a soothing ode.
As hands gently touch, a spark ignites,
Guiding us through both days and nights.

In laughter's echo, in silence's grace,
We weave our tales in this sacred space.
With every shared glance, a story unfolds,
Of dreams and wishes, of memories bold.

Together we wander in gardens of thought,
Searching for treasures that life has brought.
In the tapestry formed by each whispered word,
The essence of friendship is lovingly stirred.

Through storms and sun, we stand side by side,
In the journey of life, together we glide.
Eternal connections, like rivers, they flow,
Interwoven souls in a beautiful glow.

Gastronomy of Loving Kindness

In kitchens alive where aromas arise,
We blend our laughter, a feast for the eyes.
Tender embraces in every small bite,
Creating a world where flavors unite.

Chopping and stirring in rhythms sublime,
Each ingredient whispers the language of time.
With spices of love, we season the day,
A banquet of kindness along the way.

Tables adorned with the essence of care,
Each dish a story that we seek to share.
Through feasts we gather, our hearts all aglow,
Crafting connections in each cheerful show.

So let's raise our glasses to moments divine,
For the gastronomy of love is the finest design.
With every shared meal, we nourish the soul,
In this delightful journey, together we're whole.

The Quietude of Shared Spaces

In the hush of the room, two souls find their rest,
Comfort in silence, as life feels blessed.
The gentle brush of a hand tells the tale,
In quietude's grasp, we softly exhale.

Sunlight filters through as shadows entwine,
Creating a canvas where hearts can align.
In whispers unspoken, connections ignite,
In the tranquil embrace, we embrace the night.

Outside the chaos, a world far away,
In shared spaces found, we choose to stay.
With a glance and a smile, a bond takes its shape,
In the silence between, we quietly escape.

For in these still moments, we find our own peace,
Where love blooms gently, and worries can cease.
Within quietude shared, our spirits take flight,
In the beauty of stillness, we bask in the light.

Tides of Gentle Understanding

Whispers of the ocean breeze,
Caressing shores with gentle ease.
Hearts aligned, in rhythm's sway,
Guide us softly on our way.

With every wave that kisses land,
We find a bond, a timeless strand.
Trusting tides, we ebb and flow,
In perfect sync, our spirits grow.

Moments shared beneath the sun,
In silence, warmth, we are as one.
The world may change, but we hold fast,
Our hearts entwined, a love that lasts.

Together facing every storm,
Through gentle night, to brightest morn.
In understanding, love will thrive,
Tides of trust will keep us alive.

The Language of Loving Awareness

In glances exchanged, we find our words,
A silent dance, with whispers heard.
Each gentle touch, a heart's refrain,
In loving awareness, we feel no pain.

Our thoughts intertwine like vines so sweet,
Crafting stories with every heartbeat.
With presence, we paint colors bright,
In the canvas of love, pure delight.

Every moment a treasure shared,
In this language, we are bared.
With open hearts and listening ears,
We build a world that calms our fears.

Side by side, we light the dark,
In loving awareness, we leave our mark.
Together, we rise, with hopes anew,
In this language, it's just me and you.

Unraveling Hearts' Secrets

Beneath the surface, secrets lie,
Like whispered dreams that never die.
With gentle hands, we'll start to unfold,
The stories etched in hearts of gold.

In quiet moments, we will dare,
To share the truths that linger there.
Vulnerable, with courage bright,
We'll embrace the shadows with our light.

Layer by layer, we'll seek and find,
The hidden gems that bind our minds.
With every truth, we feel more whole,
Unraveling the depths of the soul.

Through trust and love, our hearts reveal,
The tender secrets that they conceal.
In this journey, we are free,
Unraveled hearts, in harmony.

Illuminating Pathways of Togetherness

In every step, a light will shine,
Guiding us through pathways divine.
With hands held tight, our fears will fade,
Illuminated by love's cascade.

In laughter shared, we find our way,
Together weaving night and day.
With open hearts and minds aligned,
We create a space where love's defined.

Each challenge faced, we face as one,
With warmth that outshines the bright sun.
In unity, we break the chain,
Illuminating joy, erasing pain.

As stars will guide us through the night,
In togetherness, we find our light.
With every breath, we nurture dreams,
Pathways aglow with love's bright beams.

The Radiance of Shared Moments

In laughter's glow, we find our grace,
Sunshine dances on each face.
Memories twinkle like stars above,
In every heartbeat, we feel love.

With hands entwined, we journey wide,
Through whispered dreams, side by side.
The world fades away, just us two,
In the moments shared, life feels new.

The canvas of joy in colors bright,
Together we paint, our hearts take flight.
Through storms and calm, our spirits soar,
Each shared moment opens a door.

In quiet corners, where time stands still,
We savor feelings, we embrace the thrill.
Every glance and touch ignites a spark,
In the radiance of moments, we leave our mark.

Multiplying Light Through Togetherness

In unity, we shine so bright,
Every step we take, pure delight.
Two souls intertwined, hearts aligned,
Multiplying light, love we find.

A tapestry woven of laughter and tears,
Through the passage of days and years.
In each other's arms, the shadows fade,
Together, the foundation of joy is laid.

In the stillness, our spirits sing,
The warmth of your touch, my heart's spring.
Every moment cherished, every glance a ray,
Together we light up the darkest day.

Through shared journeys, we explore the night,
Hand in hand, multiplying light.
With every breath, in sync we flow,
In togetherness, our love does grow.

Serene Reflections of Mutual Love

In tranquil waters, our hearts reflect,
Silent whispers of love perfect.
Each gentle wave, a soothing balm,
In serene moments, we feel calm.

Beneath the stars, our dreams align,
In the quiet, your heart meets mine.
A serene embrace, the world we greet,
In mutual love, we find our beat.

With every sunrise, a fresh new view,
Our reflections dance, forever true.
In peaceful pauses, our souls connect,
Together in love, we softly reflect.

Through every challenge, every stride,
In the shadows, we still reside.
With tranquil hearts, our love will swell,
In serene reflections, all is well.

The Artistry of Heartfelt Communication

In every word, a story unfolds,
Of passions deep and hearts bold.
With gentle tones and vibrant hues,
The artistry of love we choose.

Through laughter's melody and whispers sweet,
Every moment shared, a blend of heat.
With open hearts and listening ears,
We craft our tale through hopes and fears.

The brush of silence speaks so loud,
In tender glances, we feel proud.
With unspoken truths, we bridge the gap,
In the dance of words, our love's a map.

In heartfelt communication, we refine,
The artistry of our love divine.
With every note, together we compose,
A symphony of feelings that ever grows.

Illuminated Paths of Connection

Shadows fade in the golden light,
Hearts align, their rhythms bright.
Words unspoken, spirits soar,
Together we find what we explore.

Gentle whispers guide our way,
In the silence, we choose to stay.
Every glance, a story shared,
In this dance, nothing is spared.

Through the trees, we walk as one,
Finding joy in the rising sun.
With every step, a bond we weave,
In this moment, we believe.

Hand in hand, we journey far,
Love's embrace, our guiding star.
In the night, the glow remains,
Illuminated paths, no more chains.

The Art of Tender Presence

In quiet moments, hearts unfold,
The art of listening, stories told.
A gentle touch, a knowing smile,
Presence felt, though still awhile.

Breath intertwines, a sacred space,
In your eyes, I find my place.
Every heartbeat, a rhythm shared,
In tender silence, love declared.

Hands held softly, warmth intense,
In stillness lies our recompense.
As time drifts forth, we linger near,
In the art of presence, all is clear.

With you, the world fades away,
Together we are night and day.
In each moment, a new dawn breaks,
The art of love, all it takes.

Sacred Embrace of Togetherness

Underneath the starlit skies,
Love blossoms where the spirit flies.
In your arms, a refuge found,
A sacred bond, in silence crowned.

Laughter dances through the air,
Joy entwined in every care.
In this space, we find our grace,
The sacred embrace we can't replace.

Through storms that come, we stand as one,
Facing fears until they're done.
In unity, we rise and fall,
The strength of love, it conquers all.

Every heartbeat sings the tune,
In our lives, the sun and moon.
Togetherness, a glowing frame,
In this embrace, we weave our name.

The Light Within Two

In the dawn, a shimmer bright,
Two souls merging, pure delight.
With every smile, a spark ignites,
The light within, our shared flights.

In gentle breezes, whispers play,
Creating dreams that guide our way.
Through the shadows, we will shine,
Illuminating paths, all divine.

Every heartbeat, a symphony,
Resonating in harmony.
In each moment, love casts its glow,
The light within two, forever flow.

Together we rise, bright as fire,
In our bond, we climb higher.
In this journey, we will find,
The light of love, forever kind.

Whispers of Heartstrings

In quiet corners, secrets blend,
Soft echoes where our hearts descend.
A gentle sigh, a tender glance,
In whispered tones, our souls entrance.

Beneath the stars, our shadows twine,
With every breath, our fates align.
The night unveils what words won't say,
In silence, love finds its own way.

Amidst the chaos, stillness reigns,
In heart's embrace, we break the chains.
A melody that time forgot,
In heartstrings' grip, we weave our plot.

For in each note, a story starts,
The symphony of yearning hearts.
Together we dance, a sacred beat,
In whispers sweet, our love's retreat.

Embracing the Radiant Soul

In morning light, your laughter glows,
A vibrant hue where warmth bestows.
With every hug, the world feels bright,
In your embrace, I find my light.

The sun ignites the skies we trace,
In radiant joy, we find our space.
A gentle spark in every glance,
Together we live, a wondrous dance.

Through shadows long, our spirits soar,
Embracing love, we ask for more.
The universe conspired right,
In your embrace, I find my flight.

With every dream, I see you near,
The soul's reflection, crystal clear.
In harmony, we're intertwined,
Embracing the magic, love defined.

Love's Gentle Awakening

In softest dawn, our hearts emerge,
With subtle warmth, sweet feelings surge.
A gentle touch, a knowing smile,
In love's embrace, we stay awhile.

The world awakens, whispers fall,
In tender moments, we hear the call.
A quiet promise in every breath,
In love's cocoon, we conquer death.

Through every storm, together strong,
With whispered hopes, we hum our song.
A journey new, where dreams take flight,
In love's gentle wake, all feels right.

As petals bloom and tides will churn,
In love's sweet flame, our hearts will burn.
Forever changed by what we've found,
In gentle waking, love is profound.

Alchemy of Affection

In whispered words, our hearts combine,
With every glance, a spark divine.
We touch the gold in simple days,
In alchemy, our passion plays.

Through trials faced, love finds its way,
In every laugh and tear we sway.
The magic feels like ancient art,
Transforming shadows, heart to heart.

With potion brewed from trust and care,
We mix our dreams in tender air.
The warmth of hands, a loving trace,
In every moment, we find our grace.

For in this blend, we find our home,
In shared concoctions, never alone.
Together we dance through life's array,
In love's alchemy, we are the way.

Flowing Rivers of Understanding

In gentle bends, the waters flow,
Whispers of truth in soft undertow.
Through valleys wide, and mountains high,
We search for answers, asking why.

The currents share their sacred tales,
Of love and hope that never fails.
With every splash, a bond is made,
In harmony, our fears allayed.

As rivers meet, so hearts unite,
In flowing streams, we find our light.
Embracing all with open arms,
In understanding, we find our charms.

Together, we will forge a path,
Through torrential storms and gentle bath.
With empathy, our spirits rise,
In flowing rivers, wisdom lies.

The Warmth of Genuine Embrace

In twilight's glow, two souls entwine,
The warmth of love, a sacred sign.
With outstretched arms, we draw so near,
In every heartbeat, silence clear.

A gentle touch, a knowing smile,
In this embrace, the world feels mild.
As whispers float upon the air,
A promise made, beyond compare.

Through trials faced, we stand as one,
In every struggle, hope's begun.
With every hug, a life's embrace,
In genuine love, we find our place.

In tender moments, we are whole,
Two beating hearts in sync, our goal.
Together, through whatever comes,
In genuine embrace, love hums.

A Canvas of Harmonious Souls

Upon the canvas, colors blend,
In shades of joy, our sorrows mend.
With brushstrokes light, we paint our dreams,
In each created space, love beams.

With every hue, a story told,
Of brave hearts and spirits bold.
In vibrant tones, our essence glows,
A masterpiece where kindness grows.

We intertwine in radiant grace,
As melodies in soft embrace.
Together, we compose our song,
In harmonious dance, we belong.

Each soul a shade, unique and bright,
In every struggle, find the light.
A canvas vast, we all partake,
Creating beauty, hearts awake.

Echoes of Peaceful Hearts

In quiet corners where shadows play,
Resides a calm at end of day.
Echoes dance on softened air,
Whispering truths beyond compare.

With every beat, a tranquil sound,
In peaceful hearts, our hopes abound.
Like gentle rivers, we flow free,
Together forging unity.

Through trials faced and storms we brave,
Our bond is strong, and love will save.
In every silence, peace unfolds,
A harmony that never molds.

In whispered dreams, we find our way,
With echoes bright that softly sway.
In peaceful hearts, we come alive,
In shared existence, we will thrive.

9 789916 871393